LEOŠ JANÁČEK

SINFONIETTA

Edited by/Herausgegeben von
Jarmil Burghauser

Ernst Eulenburg Ltd

London · Mainz · Madrid · New York · Paris · Tokyo · Toronto · Zürich

LEOŠ JANÁČEK

Sinfonietta

Leoš Janáček (1854–1928) achieved sudden fame in 1916 after the enormous success of *Jenufa* in Prague that year. The opera was staged in rapid succession in all the main European opera houses, and this provided the stimulus for a remarkable upsurge of creative activity on the part of the composer. Janáček, until now practically unknown yet on the threshold of old age, began to compose one work after another, mostly operas, but also much symphonic, choral and chamber music.

If his symphonic rhapsody *Taras Bulba*, written during the first war, expresses his firm hope in the final victory of his nation in its struggle for liberty, his *Sinfonietta* (1926) reflects the joy of the happily-developing life in the restored state, joy invigorated also by the composer's newly revived intimate feelings.

The work resulted from a rather insignificant impulse – a commission to write fanfares for the planned 'general exercise' (*slet*) of the famous gymnastic organisation *Sokol*. (Janáček recalls a pleasant experience from the charming small town of Písek in Southern Bohemia where he appreciated an interesting, almost theatrically effective art – fanfares played by a military band during a garden festival.) Within only three weeks this germ (the first movement of the work) had grown into a five-movement cyclic composition in which the composer, according to his own words, describes 'a man of today, free, fair and joyful, with a strength and will to fight for his day'. Janáček's later explanations, though, show that he also imbued the composition with a number of recollections and impressions originating from earlier periods in his life. The later movements appertain to Brno, the capital of Moravia, where he lived for the whole of the latter part of his career.

In the second movement ('Castle' in one of the composer's aphoristic descriptions) elements of the folk dance stand in opposition to passages of majestic power. The third movement ('Convent') recalls moments when the boy Janáček – chorister and ward of the Queen's Convent at Old Brno – felt 'sacred peace . . ., nocturnal shadows and the breath of the green hill'. The fourth movement ('The street') conceived as a racy scherzo with insistent repetitions of the principal theme, may be an echo of the vivid bustle in the regenerated town. The fifth movement ('Town Hall') depicts the transformation of the historical centre of the city, formerly the focus of the oppression of the past, nto the place which reflected and personified the sovereignty of the people. During the closing section of the work the fanfares of the first movement reappear; they are garlanded with trills, evoking the idea of fluttering flags.

The work was first performed on 26 June 1926 in Prague at a concert given by the Czech Philharmonic Orchestra conducted by Václav Talich; the first performance outside Czechoslovakia probably took place in New York in March 1927 (with Otto Klemperer). The score was first published in 1927 by Universal Edition, Vienna.

The present edition incorporates the corrections of palpable misprints in the first edition, realizes a number of the composer's wishes which he expressed in his letters to Universal Edition (but were ignored in their edition), and corrects, after the autograph in the Janáček Archives in Brno, some errors which were made by the first copyist and overlooked by the composer: e.g. the mutual displacement of the cellos and double-basses in bars 47–50 of the second movement; the erroneous assigning of a part to a fourth trombone whereas the composer wanted only three trombones and a tuba throughout.

Some of the original metronome marks have been omitted where they are doubtful (the composer owned a defective apparatus and often changed his mind about speeds). The D flat common chord for the nine trumpets in the last three bars of the work is inserted in accordance with tradition, although it is absent in the primary sources.

The work is notated in accordance with the editorial principles of the *Complete Critical Edition* of Janáček's works, especially in the use of accidentals, choice of enharmonic notes and time-signatures, thus clarifying the composer's intentions.

Jarmil Burghauser, 1978

LEOŠ JANÁČEK

Sinfonietta

Durch den enormen Erfolg der 1916 in Prag aufgeführten Oper *Jenufa* wurde Leoš Janáček (1854–1928) plötzlich berühmt. Das Werk wurde bald darauf in allen bedeutenden Opernhäusern Europas inszeniert, und dadurch wurde der Komponist zu einer neuen, ausserordentlich produktiven, schöpferischen Tätigkeit angeregt. Damals schon im vorgeschrittenen Alter und vorher praktisch unbekannt, begann Janáček nun ein Werk nach dem anderen zu komponieren; hauptsächlich waren es Opern, doch schrieb er auch viel sinfonische Musik, sowie Chor- und Kammermusikwerke.

Während seine, im ersten Weltkreig entstandene sinfonische Rhapsodie *Taras Bulba* die feste Hoffnung auf den Endsieg seiner Nation im Kampf um die Freiheit ausdrückt, schildert seine *Sinfonietta* (1926) die durch das sich glücklich entwickelnde Leben im wiederhergestellten Staat entstandene Freude, welcher ihrerseits durch die neu erweckten intimen Gefühle des Komponisten ebenfalls Kräfte zuflossen.

Der Anlas zur Komposition dieses Werks war ein ziemlich unbedeutender Auftrag, Fanfaren für die geplante ‚Generalübung' (*slet*) des berühmten Turnvereins *Sokol* zu schreiben. (Janáček hat erzählt, wie er in der hübschen südböhmischen Stadt Písek die Freude hatte, der interessanten, gleichsam bühnenmässig wirksamen Darstellung einer Militärkapelle beizuwohnen, die während eines Gartenfestes Fanfaren spielte.) Innerhalb von nur drei Wochen war aus dieser Keimzelle (dem ersten Satz des Werks) eine zyklische Komposition in fünf Sätzen geworden, in welcher der Komponist, seinen eigenen Worten nach, ‚einen Menschen von heute' beschreibt, der, frei, redlich und froh ist, und der den Willen und die Kraft hat, für sein Dasein zu kämpfen'. Allerdings beweisen Erklärungen, die Janáček später gegeben hat, dass das Werk auch auf gewissen Erinnerungen und Eindrücken beruht, die aus den früheren Zeiten seines Lebens stammen. Die letzten Sätze stehen mit Brno, der Hauptstadt von Mähren, in Verbindung, in welcher er sein ganzes späteres Leben verbrachte.

Im zweiten Satz (in einer der aphoristischen Beschreibungen des Komponisten als ‚Burg' bezeichnet) stehen Elemente des Volktanzes im Gegensatz zu starken, majestätischen Passagen. Der dritte Satz (‚Kloster') erinnert an die Zeit, in der Janáček Chorknabe war und unter der Vormundschaft des Königinnenklosters im alten Brno stand, als er ‚heiligen Frieden . . .' empfand, und ‚nächtliche Schatten, und den Hauch des grünen Hügels' wahrnahm. Der vierte Satz (‚die Strasse'), der als zügiges Scherzo mit immerwiederkehrenden Wiederholungen des Hauptthemas gestaltet wurde, mag als ein Echo der lebhaften Geschäftigkeit in der wiedergeborenen Stadt angesehen werden. Der fünfte Satz (‚Rathaus') beschreibt die Verwandlung des historischen Stadtzentrums von einem früheren Brennpunkt der Unterdrückung zu einem Platz, der die Oberhoheit des Volkes symbolisiert. Im letzten Teil des Werks erklingen noch einmal die Fanfaren aus dem ersten Satz, diesmal mit Trillern umwoben, die an das Flattern der Fahnen erinnern.

Das Werk wurde erstmalig am 26. Juni 1926 in Prag, in einem Konzert des Tschechischen Philharmonischen Orchesters unter der Leitung von Václav Talich aufgeführt. Die erste Aufführung ausserhalb der Tschechoslowakei fand wahrscheinlich im März 1927 in New York (unter der Leitung von Otto Klemperer) statt. Die Erstausgabe der Partitur erschien 1927 bei der Universal Edition in Wien.

Die vorliegende Ausgabe enthält die Berichtigung offensichtlicher Druckfehler in der Erstausgabe und trägt gewissen Wünschen des Komponisten Rechnung, die er in seinen Briefen an die Universal Edition ausgedrückt hat (die aber in der genannten Ausgabe nicht berücksichtigt worden sind). Ausserdem wurden, auf Grund des im Janáček-Archiv in Brno befindlichen Autographs, einige Fehler berichtigt, die vom ersten Kopisten gemacht, und vom Komponisten übersehen worden waren, z.B. die Auswechslung von Celli und Bässen in den Takten 47–50 im zweiten Satz, und die irrtümliche Angabe einer vierten Posaunenstimme, obwohl der Komponist durchweg nur drei Posaunen und eine Tuba verlangt hat.

In Zweifelsfällen sind einige der ursprünglichen Metronomangaben fortgelassen worden (der Komponist besass ein schadhaftes Metronom und änderte oft seine Meinung über die Geschwindigkeit der Tempi). Der traditionsgemäss von den neun Trompeten gespielte Des-Dur Akkord in den letzten drei Takten des Werks wurde hinzugefügt, obwohl er nicht in den Hauptquellen steht.

Die Notierung entspricht dem in der *kritischen Gesamtausgabe* der Werke Janáčeks angewendeten Prinzips, vor allem im Gebrauch der Vorzeichen, der Wahl der enharmonischen Noten und der Zeitmasse, wodurch die Absichten des Komponisten verdeutlicht werden.

Jarmil Burghauser, 1978
Deutsche Übersetzung Stefan de Haan

ORCHESTRA

4	Flutes (4th doubling Piccolo)
2	Oboes
	Cor anglais
	Clarinet (E♭)
2	Clarinets (B♭)
	Bass Clarinet (B♭)
2	Bassoons
4	Horns (F)
3	Trumpets (F)
3	Trombones
	Tuba
9	Trumpets (C)
2	Tenor Tubas
2	Bass Trumpets (B♭)

Timpani
Percussion

Harp

Strings

Duration/Aufführungsdauer: 25 Min.

SINFONIETTA

I

Leoš Janáček
1854-1928

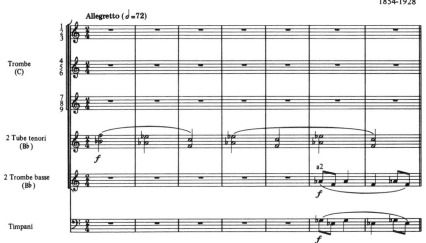

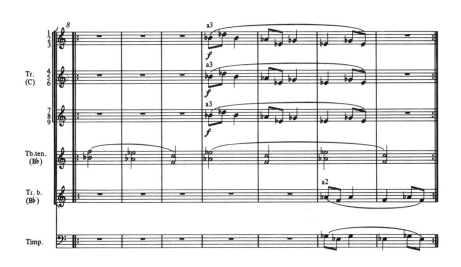

No. 1369　　　　　EE 6669　　　　　Ernst Eulenburg Ltd

4

6

II

10

14

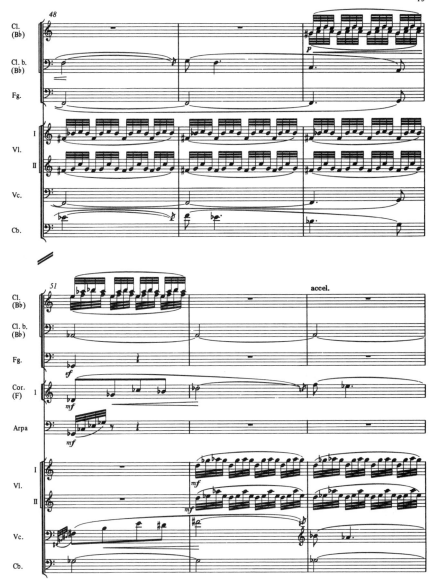

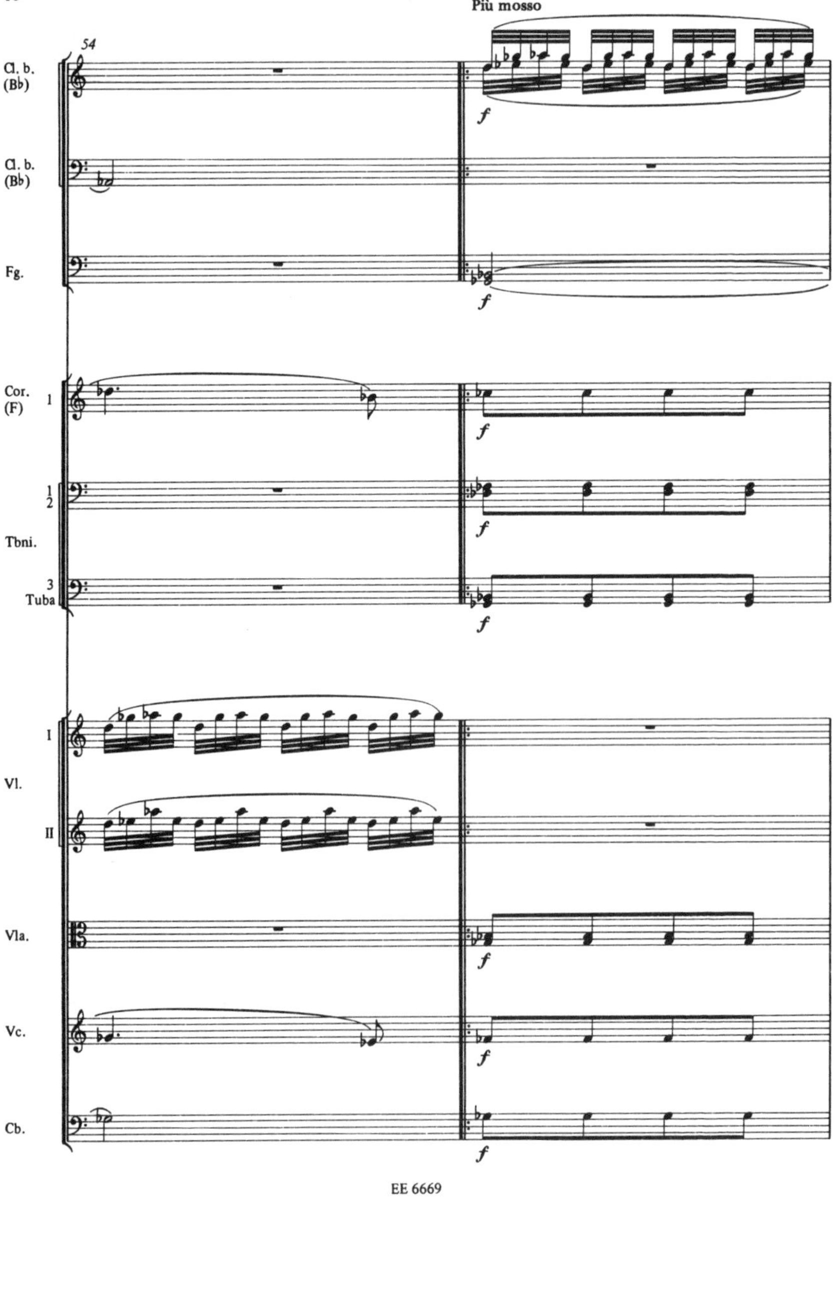
Più mosso
54
Cl. b. (B♭)
Cl. b. (B♭)
Fg.
Cor. (F) 1
1 2
Tbni.
3 Tuba
I
Vl.
II
Vla.
Vc.
Cb.
f

20

EE 6669

24

EE 6669

26

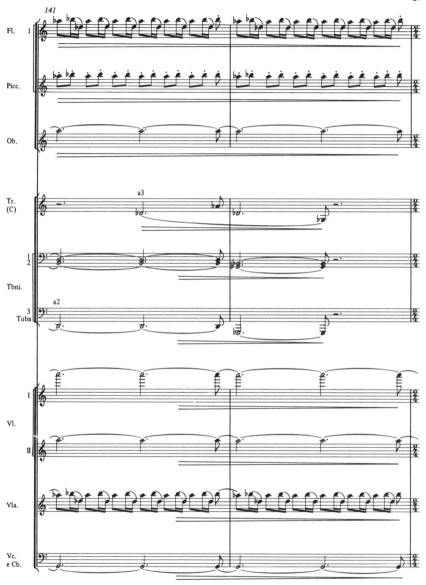

28

158

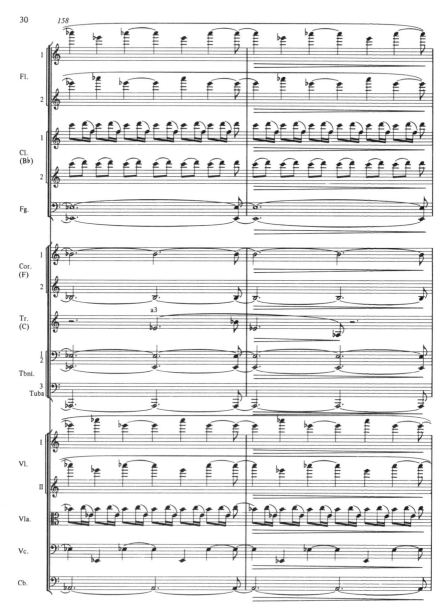

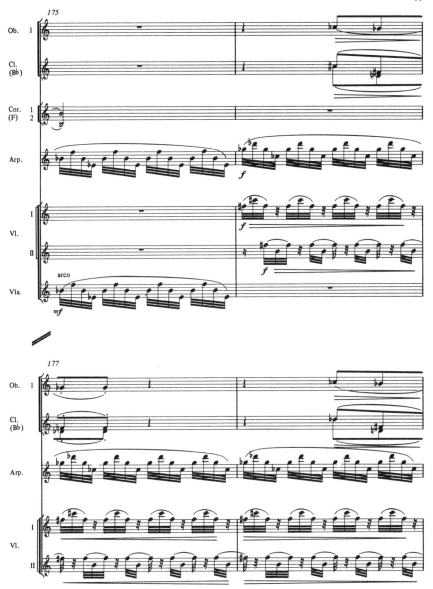

EE 6669

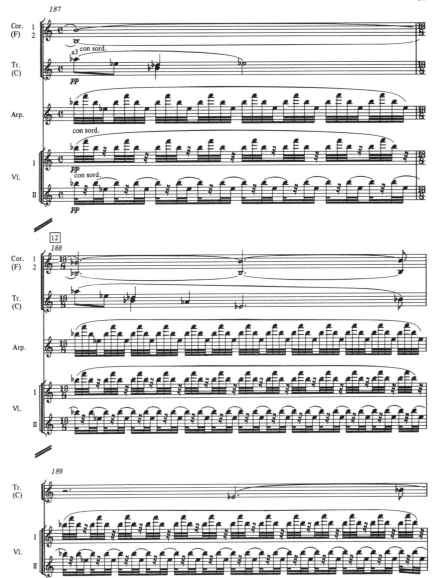

III

42

EE 6669

EE 6669

46

48

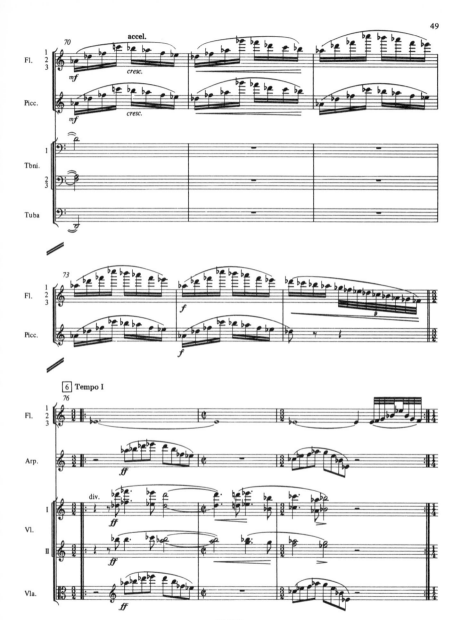

54

EE 6669

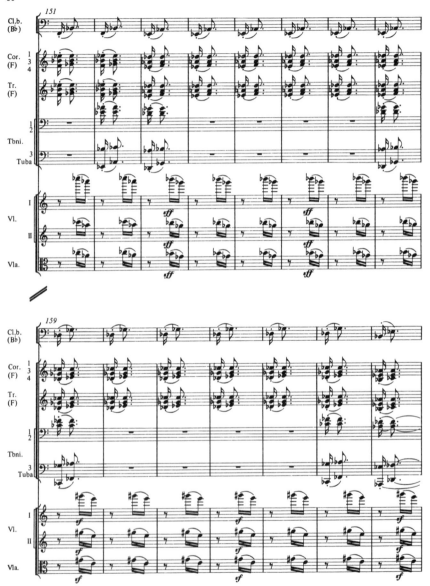

EE 6669

IV

66

74

EE 6669

Prestissimo

V

EF. 6669

84

86

92

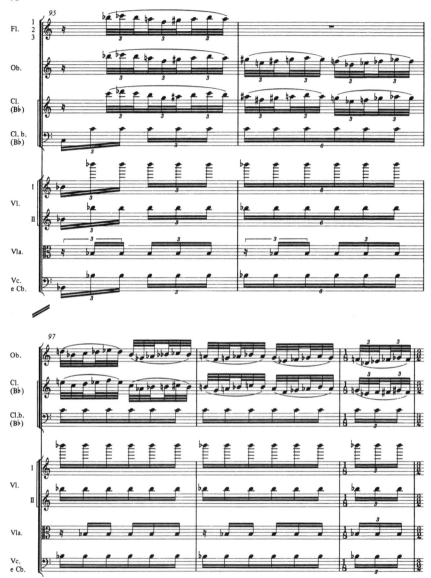

EE 6669

94

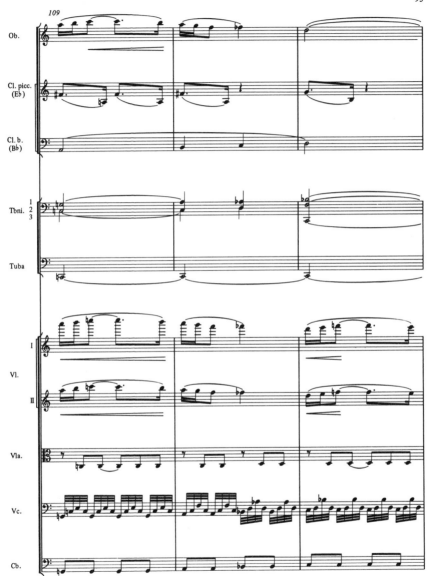

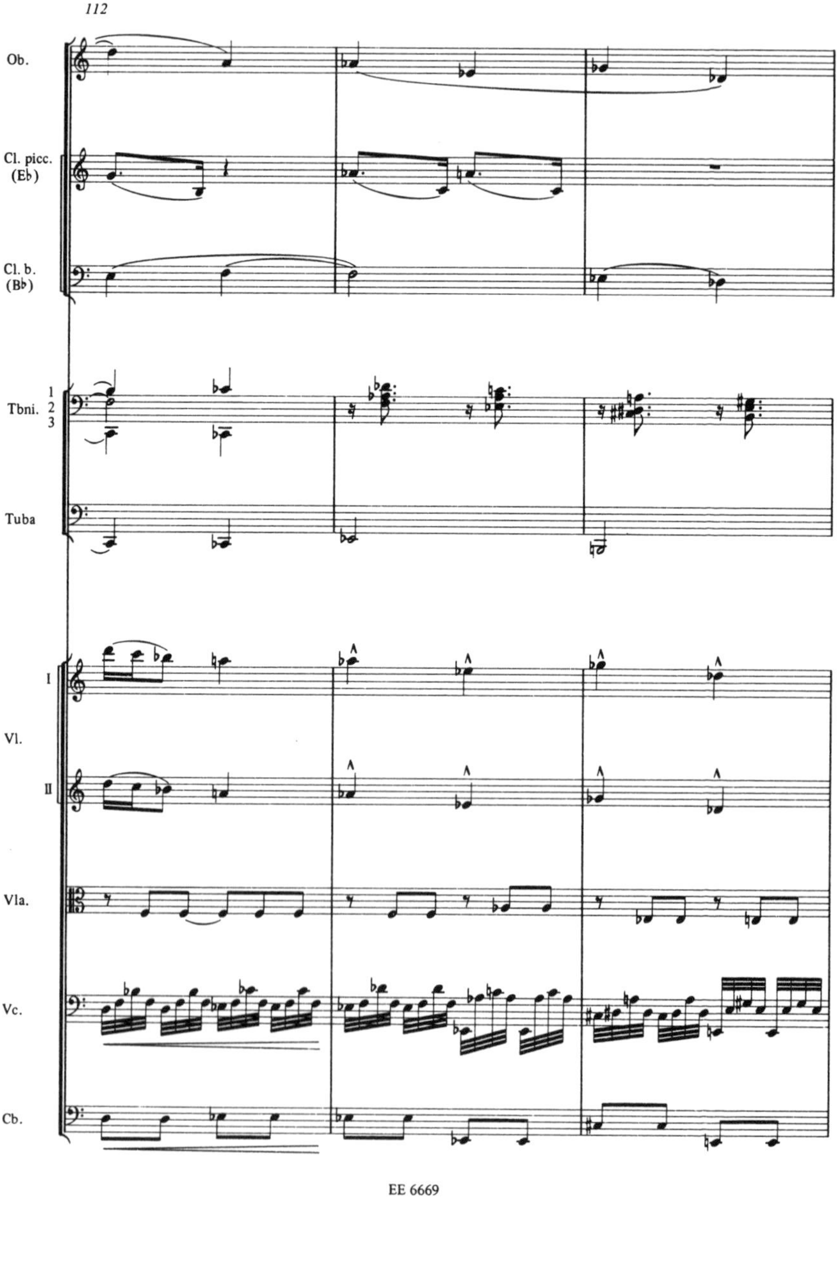
112
Ob.
Cl. picc. (E♭)
Cl. b. (B♭)
1
2
3
Tbni.
Tuba
I
Vl.
II
Vla.
Vc.
Cb.

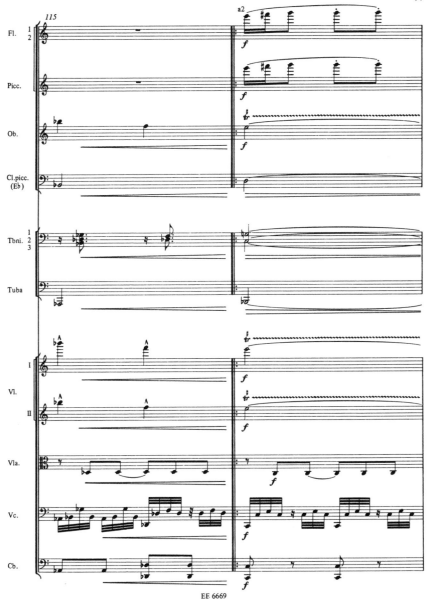

102

104

Allegro (♩. =72)

177

112

EE 6669